*Romancing Your Muse* Book 1

Writing Inspiration Through Mindful Walking

Kathleen Shoop & Lori M. Jones
with Madhu Bazaz Wangu

Copyright © 2021 Kathleen Shoop

All Rights Reserved

Year of the Book
135 Glen Avenue
Glen Rock, PA 17327

ISBN: 978-1-64649-195-7 (print)

ISBN: 978-1-64649-196-4 (ebook)

No part of this publication may be reproduced, distributed, or transmitted in any form or by any means, including photocopying, recording, or other electronic or mechanical methods, without the prior written permission of the publisher, except in the case of brief quotations embodied in critical reviews and certain other noncommercial uses permitted by copyright law.

Permission generously granted by author Sarah Waters and her agency for quotation on page 32.

Contents

Introduction 1

The Spirit Soars ~ The Problem is Solved 11

Step 1 ~ Step 2 ~ Step 3 17

Cleanse the Palate 23

Plant the Seed ~ Water the Sprout 27

Emotional Journey 35

A Writer's High 45

Unglued 49

Exercise for Mental & Writing Health 55

Zen and the Art of Cognitive Maintenance 61

Waiting for the Weather 65

Walking with Company 73

So You Can't Walk… 71

Getting Started 81

The Bridge 85

Poems *by Madhu Wangu* 91

Me thinks that the moment
my legs begin to move,
my thoughts begin to flow.

~Henry David Thoreau

Introduction

This small book began as an introductory guide for those attending the first Mindful Writers Retreat in Fall 2014 to introduce them to the concept of Mindful Walking. The retreat is comprised of several elements: sustained writing, sitting meditation, walking meditation, and communal meals. After six years and fourteen retreats, we are offering this updated version of Writing Inspiration Through Mindful Walking to fiction and nonfiction writers everywhere.

Having the opportunity to engage with other mindful writers generates inspiration that lasts far beyond our time at the retreat center. But we hope this book will encourage writers to pull retreat elements into their daily writing practice, to use walking meditation to inspire more and richer writing even when alone.

Mirroring the retreat experience at home is a goal for many mindful writers. Before we dig into mindful walking we want to present some background on how two elements of the Mindful Writers Retreats developed.

One element of the retreats was born of the wisdom and practice of Madhu Bazzaz Wangu, Ph.D.

Beginning over a decade ago, after a lifetime of meditating and writing alone, Madhu invited writers to join her and learn the tool that had transformed her writing life. Set in a room at a restaurant, Madhu's sitting meditations, followed by hours of writing, proved powerful even despite distractions in the restaurant. The room tries to be private with its glass doors separating the mindful writers from the happy eaters just a few feet away. But even as the scent of pancakes and bacon waft into the "cloistered" room, even as a child screeches for his milk just beyond the door, authors find Madhu's calming voice and her illustrative cues lure them into the most productive writing of their week.

Successful writing in that semi-public setting speaks to the impact of Madhu's guidance. The practice she so generously shares is potent. This book contains some of her poetry and you can listen to her Meditations for Mindful Writers on YouTube, download them from iTunes, or join her on Facebook at Mindful Writers Online.

As you work through this book, feel free to bookmark and use Madhu's collection of poems, clustered at the end, as inspiration for sitting meditation. Or you can borrow pieces and lines for a meditative mantra.

And that brings us to the second type of meditation that helps writers hone their work at the retreat and at home – walking meditation. This practice diverges from sitting meditation in several ways, but most notable is that walking meditation requires each person to move at one's own pace, to find the length of stride and speed that allows optimal meditation.

Because of the difference in fitness level, experience with walking mediation, and the terrain, walking meditation is not guided in the same way that Madhu guides sitting meditation in person or through her recordings.

This book includes snapshots of how mindful walkers begin, what they experience, and some of the science and spirituality that undergirds the process.

When adding walking to your writing practice – whether at home or on a retreat – keep a few things in mind. Wear comfortable shoes and select a safe place to walk. Don't head out on a busy road with a narrow, cinder-laden berm and expect to be able to let your mind focus on your body, your breath, your book. You'll be too busy dodging careless drivers and making sure you don't twist an ankle to allow your mind to unravel plot problems.

Likewise, mountainous or rocky terrain could force your attention to safety issues. Seasoned moving meditators may be automated and comfortable enough with their agility that they can access a meditative state while engaged in intricate movements, but most would rather stick to places that are safe and easy. Before we get into the meat of the book, the following introductions offer a sense of who Lori and Kathie are and how each came to use walking meditation as a tool to enhance every part of their writing lives.

Kathie's Story...

My first experiences with meditation happened accidentally. I was on swim team as a kid. Hours and hours in a pool produced my first opportunity to see how repetitive movements (like running, walking, drawing, swimming, knitting, and more!) could create an environment that allowed my mind to run free, to problem solve, to find unexpected answers to troubling questions.

In college, I turned to running and had the same experience as with swimming. I would emerge from an hour of running ready to tackle the day. These days I mostly walk and take spin classes. Both help me reach a meditative state that heightens my writing quality and increases volume.

I've known the value of these meditative experiences since I was fourteen, but I did not apply the label of meditation to the process until I began working with Madhu Wangu.

It didn't take many sessions with the group at Eat'n

Park for me to begin to make the connection between what happened when I would walk or run to what happened with Madhu.

Sitting meditation – the guided words and soothing voice of Madhu – creates an internal environment that enriches my writing as a whole, in ways that I don't expect until I'm writing. It develops me as a person and then that work spills into my writing.

Walking meditation provides the chance to pinpoint writing issues and manuscript problems, then solve them in a way that staring at the computer screen does not.

I am fortunate to have been able to experience both sitting and walking meditation. Each practice works with the other, creating an environment that encourages me to fully engage in writing craft, to put aside whatever I can't control in the business end of my writing career.

Lori's Story...

My writing journey began following the birth of my first daughter. I'd made up a fairy tale and would tell it to her daily. I finally wrote it down. It wasn't until I wrote a story for my second daughter, Riley, following her surgery to get a pacemaker, that I'd get one of my stories published.

Riley's Heart Machine received a contract in 2009. I loved crafting children's stories, but my true joy and fulfillment was realized when I took a shot at women's fiction in November 2009. I'm now about to finish my fifth novel.

I have tried to walk away from it, to quit this madness that we writers embark on, but I can't and won't. Writing has become an integral part of me. It's my way of expressing my feelings and finding contentment.

I was introduced to writing meditation with Madhu Wangu. That experience took my writing life to the next level. I became more aware of how my mind and body affected my creativity and I became more disciplined in controlling it.

This then spilled over into my workouts. For me, I had probably been experiencing the benefits of mindful movement for years, but wasn't aware of it. I consciously recognized it around the time I wrote my first novel.

When I would go for a run, I began hearing my characters' voices and getting ideas for scenes. Over the years, I've been able to tune into my ability to foster creativity during long runs and walks. I would also use my running and walking time for prayer or to release stress.

I now consciously use my running and walking time to relax, focus, turn inward, and hone my writing creativity. Often, I will refer to my "run," but typically I alternate running and walking. Most of my meditation and creative flow occur during my walking time.

My bottom line: blood flow equals creative flow. Releasing stress and worldly worries allows the ideas to blossom.

Thoughts come clearly
while one walks.

~*Thomas Mann*

Meditative movement is a process that can coax writers and artists of all types into a state of inspiration, a state that can fuel and deepen your work. Experts in the fields of science and spirituality spend their lives studying and discussing what happens when a person moves in a repetitive and fluid manner. Some of those ideas will be explored here as they pertain to writing and writers.

Walking is a good example of the type of movement that can fan the creative flames. Presented here are thoughts that countless writers have shared regarding their schedules and the vital role that daily walks play in the value and volume of output. This book will offer glimpses into the hearts and minds of those who've discovered that walking meditation has inspired their work, and who've found that movement feels like magic.

The Spirit Soars
~ The Problem is Solved

In the early stages of exploring literature pertaining to mindful movement, several philosophies emerged. Two of these mindful walking "types" will be central to this book. One is called *slow walking* (see Resources list for Thich Nhat Hanh). The other experience – which, to our knowledge, has not been formally named by a particular practitioner – doesn't specify a speed (it could very well be slow walking) but it embodies a more purposeful goal: to solve manuscript problems.

A *slow walking* experience draws a writer's attention to his body, to the movement itself, and the environment around him. Hanh suggests, "[…] we do not put anything ahead of ourselves and run after it."

Another type of walking meditation makes room for seeking solutions, for deepening one's work-in-progress. Its movement begins like slow walking, but there is a seed sown, a problem to be mulled and done away with.

Let's look at slow walking meditation for a moment. Thich Nhat Hanh, a Buddhist Monk, suggests a mindful life: whether walking, eating, sitting, or socializing, we should be mindful and present. He suggests that an acute awareness, especially as experienced in mindful walking, will lead to happiness, will reveal abundance in what we have in life instead of yearning for all that is out of reach. The peace and tranquility found with this type of meditation can be an exceptional state in which to approach the keyboard.

This idea of happiness being linked to mindfulness, to walking, connects with what the authors have found in terms of movement. This moving meditation can absolutely inspire a writer's work.

Slow meditative walking, being present, feeling the wonder of air pressed against skin, noticing a balding tree, chirping birds, the thick scent of roses, is sometimes all that is needed to prepare for writing.

In addition to the spiritual rewards that Hanh suggests slow walking meditation will provide, there is hard science connecting fluid movement to increased creativity, to paths over, through and around obstacles. Findings demonstrate that in the midst of the walking, problems are untangled, solutions are found. There is overlap between what is experienced in mindful movement as it relates to science and the spirit. Both will be discussed.

There are times when the most important thing a writer needs to do when walking is to connect with a higher power – the universe, his inner-self, whatever it is that brings inspiration. There are other times when walking inspires a mental miracle, a faucet gushing forth with multiple answers to the worst writing obstacles.

For practiced mindful walkers, accessing the space where their muse lives is nearly automatic. It's tethered to walking like a tooth rooted in a mouth. Practice helps, but many writers report that their first time out mindful walking resulted in the production of entire scenes, the unknotting of snarled plots, revelations of the exact way a character should argue with the protagonist.

For Kathie, her walks allow minute details to be born. For instance, walking showed her that her character Rose in *After the Fog*, should toss her hands through the air while bickering instead of being balled at her side as she'd originally written. Suddenly, it's clear. The character is further developed and more tightly tied to the person Kathie meant to create—a tiny development that changed everything for writer and reader. Both spiritual and creative inspiration come when writers experience moving meditation. It can change process, product, and person in profound ways.

There will be days when walking meditation feeds the spirit and other times when it feeds the work. Most outings will find the author returning to the computer having experienced writing and spiritual inspiration. Writing improves dramatically once authors give over to movement as a means to ignite and funnel inspiration.

Creative Action Part 1:

Think of all the areas where you can venture on your walks. Obviously around your neighborhood is the most practical, but also think of nearby wooded acres or parks you can explore. Maybe when you have the time, you can drive to a new park or trail. Have a few different places planned that will offer a variety of experiences such as streams or water sources, wooded areas, foot bridges, and other natural beauties and wonders. While it is the outdoor experience and repetition of movement that will trigger the creative juices, adding in nature's beauty will enhance your experience.

Creative Action Part 2:

Come up with a few mantras that speak to you. Write them down and memorize your favorite ones. They can be about nature, walking, or self-reflective. Anything that you can repeat when your mind starts to go off-course during your walks.

Lori likes:

I give to the universe, and the universe gives to me.

And, the go-to one we reference often in this book can also be used when distracted:

Back to the body. Back to the breath. Back to the book.

Start writing some of your own and see what happens!

Walks.
The body advances,
while the mind flutters
around like a bird.

~Jules Renard

Inhale (Step 1 ~ Step 2 ~ Step 3) Exhale (1 ~ 2 ~3)

In researching walking as it pertains to writing and meditation, numerous contradictions were noted. The body of peer-reviewed studies, theological musings, anecdotal evidence and snapshots into how walking engages one's muse is rich, but often contrary.

The contradictory suggestions for how to bring about peace, joy, and inspiration may seem confusing to read, but these contradictions are what kick open the process so that everyone has space to find their personal sweet spot – the place where inspiration resides and can be found nearly at will.

One facet of movement as meditation that is widely practiced is that which Thich Nhat Hanh advocates: Slow meditative walking. This can be very useful in encouraging an author to center herself, find peace, find joy. This slow, meditative walking allows tranquility and happiness to shine from inside out.

How does this happen? Hanh suggests that people focus on footfalls, breath, and nature. This allows the walker to stay present. This condition of being, of that being "enough," flushes away soot-like emotional baggage – the kind that clogs the spirit and stops writers from living the lives they desire. Hanh suggests repeating words while moving. "Lotus flower. Lotus flower blooms."

Hearing the flap of a bird's wing as it takes to the air, the sound a squirrel makes when scratching up a tree to his nest, the inhalation of the last remnants of a bonfire – the attention to these things can clear the mind for writing. Hanh suggests stopping and paying close attention to these happenings as they're encountered.

Deep cleansing breaths and the sound of feet on a winding dirt path can unravel knotted worries, cleanse away half-won arguments, and stale, gritty resentment, leaving an author ready to write. At this juncture calmness, openness, and joy that may not be duplicated in other ways are present.

Lori has found that these rhythms—noticing breath and body in a variety of ways—provide a path to writing mindfulness. She and other seasoned runners and walkers know that in order to keep breathing under control, exhaling on every other right footfall helps.

When running, if Lori's breath becomes erratic, she returns her attention to her footfalls, allowing her to control her breath. After much practice, this becomes second nature.

Creative Action—Stretch and Prepare:

First, make sure you have a small notebook and pen (or phone with the note app) to take with you on your walk. Before you venture out of your home to walk, start off with some light stretching and breathing. This will set the tone and focus for your walk. Stretch in the same order each time, so you can establish a routine.

- Neck rolls, wrist rolls, ankle rolls.
- Breathe in while stretching arms in wide circle, upward. Then exhale, while returning arms to side. Repeat several times. Focus on your breath.
- On the last arms stretch, reach down to your feet. Remain there and breathe. Then return to standing.

Tell yourself while stretching:

What do I need to tap into on this walk? What scene would I like to work through? What character would I like to talk to?

I am the one chosen to tell this story. No one else can tell it like I can. I'm full of gratitude for my gifts and my ability to walk and to write.

Breathe in… Breathe out… Stretch up… and down. To the side… to the other side… Breathe.

I give to the Universe

The universe gives to me.

I am writing a story worthy of being told. I deserve the joy I receive.

I am grateful for this time with nature and with myself.

I deserve the joy the comes from creating.

Let me walk. Let me breathe. Let me feel joy. Let me create.

Back to the body. Back to the breath. Back to the book.

Creative Action General Technique for During Your Walk:

If you are new to mindful walking as it ties to writing, use Lori's suggestion for synchronizing breath to pacing. For her, the one-two-three (INHALE) and one-two-three (EXHALE) fits her pace. Once her body is loose, her creativity follows suit.

She pulls a scene she wants to build or fix to mind then she gets her characters talking. If she becomes distracted, or her mind starts wandering away from her work-in-progress, she refocuses on her 1-2-3 breaths. Body—Breath—Book. This nearly always results in getting those pesky characters back to work!

Inhale (1,2,3)—Exhale (1,2,3)

Body—Breath—Book

How can I get Tom out of the house?

Above all, do not lose
your desire to walk.
Every day I walk myself
into a state of well-being
and walk away from every illness.
I have walked myself
into my best thoughts,
and I know of no thought
so burdensome that one cannot
walk away from it.

~*Søren Kierkegaard*

Cleanse the Palate

Thich Nhat Hanh is a Vietnamese Buddhist Monk who has been nominated for the Nobel Peace Prize. He has spent decades teaching and practicing slow walking meditation. He imparts the idea that mindful walking allows us to be present in the moment and that in being so, we will find peace, happiness, and feel joy and love. This palate cleansing allows writers to return to their computers with minds clear of distracting debris.

Walking meditation, focusing on breath, the lengthening of strides, the stretch that comes through loosening up as the writer proceeds deep into the walking hour, works as a scouring tool.

There are times when Kathie's eyes need to simply see the way the wind rocks the top of a tree, yet the air around *her* is still. Sometimes she follows the scent of honeysuckle or she focuses on her feet crunching over autumn leaves, the swinging of her arms as she naturally picks up speed.

Being in the present moment, Kathie's practice of noticing *her* moving through space as nature cuts its own path around her provides a sense of tranquility, of cleansing, of clearing the blackboard for new or deeper writing. Sometimes, this simple purging of excess, tangled, unproductive energy makes room for the good stuff to rush forth.

Creative Action:

Take to the woods or street. Note how your movements act in unison or in opposition to everything else around you. How do you grow heavier or lighter as you go? How does this simple movement free you and prepare you to write?

If I could not walk far and fast,
I think I should just
explode and perish.

~Charles Dickens

Plant the Seed
~ Water the Sprout

As mentioned earlier in this book, there are different philosophies about walking meditation. Kathie and Lori come to their walking meditation in a way that is in line with what Hanh might suggest (focus on being, on body, on what is in front of you) but they have discovered that walking can be purposeful *and* aimless. Each walking opportunity yields new perspective and fresh commitment to writing.

Lori and Kathie employ elements of mindful walking that focus on body and breath. But they also use it as a tool to enrich their thoughts, sharpen word choice, and ease the writing process. While they enjoy the spiritual benefits that come from all forms of meditation, they've found that mindful walking is one writing tool they couldn't live without. When a writer has driven himself into an inescapable corner, walking offers the space to find a solution to problems that seemed unsolvable while seated at the computer.

When this happens, it helps to head outside. The example below shows how elements of Hahn's meditative walking can combine with solving a problem – the two things can work together.

Creative Action:

Start your walk with eleven deep breaths, noticing the way a tree limb bows and dances in the wind, the way a mallard waddles by with her chicks trailing behind, each one plunking after the other into the river, the river turned brown by drenching rains that churned the mud, bringing it to the surface, the color of a skim latte.

Notice your heavy legs, or that the arches of your feet ache. Six more breaths, then begin to spool through the issue that's plaguing your writing.

Embed a problematic seed, or maybe even a sprout, into your mind. *Rose can't be at a bar. It's not proper. How can I get her inside drinking with the fellas AND make it "okay" that she's there?* Repeat some of the words from your writing problem as Hanh would suggest. With each footfall, the problem is named with its thick roots, holding fast, unyielding.

Continue walking. The movement of your body stills your worried mind, presents solutions, invites new ways of seeing your work, your life, yourself. *Yes, Rose can be in the bar. She just needs to go there to provide nursing care. THEN she can have a drink.*

Success. Revelations like this develop over the course of an hour-long walk. There are times that "answers" pop to mind nearly the instant the author starts walking. But often little bits are revealed over the course of the walk. Sometimes it's the last few minutes that yield the answer, as though the muse was teasing all along, just waiting to offer a reward of a solved plot problem.

Lori and Kathie are fairly certain Zen Master Thich Nhat Hanh wouldn't agree with this "planting of a problem to be solved." He would see it as contrary to walking with "wishlessness or aimlessness" (Hanh & Anh-Huong, p.15), as he suggests practitioners should. But Lori and Kathie have found that the deep meditative state is also exceptionally illuminating to their work and it arises from the very movement Hanh suggests.

In *Walking Meditation,* Hanh discusses the same phenomenon Lori and Kathie accidentally discovered decades years ago, during long sets of swimming practice or on running routes.

Being that the authors of this book aren't Zen Masters, they can't completely connect what happens in their minds as they plant a seed of a problem (and find solutions) with what Hanh suggests *should* happen, but they are quite certain they attain the state of mindfulness he *wants* them to experience.

Hanh might advise Lori and Kathie to "Pull away from this problem-oriented thinking, tend the sprouts later..." but they choose a combined approach instead.

The experience has been too powerful for them to abandon, the mined gold too valuable to leave behind, hoping they somehow remember what they found while walking. As solutions come, they record them in a notebook or phone: observations, scenes, images that have formed, voices that have risen up to be heard, the unexpected plot twist, the "correct" way to move a character through her world...

These answers come mysteriously, connected to the spiritual as much as the cerebral world, to spirit itself, God, whomever... The mystery is welcome, whatever it is or where it stems from. The one thing that is clear is that it's the walking that brings it all to bear. Don't miss the chance to capture the fruits of your meditative labors.

We aren't alone in knowing the value of this.

For example, Merlin Coverley wrote a book called *The Art of Wandering: The Writer as Walker*. One of the authors he discussed extensively was William Wordsworth. Wordsworth had devoted much of his life to walking long, winding, woodsy routes with his sister and good friends. But when the family moved to a new home, "...famously he used to compose much of his work while striding up and down the straight gravel path in his garden." This historical connection allows a fuller realization of the range and depth of what happens when practicing walking meditation.

Lori and Kathie have experimented to see if they yield the same benefits during interval-type exercises or boot camp workouts. Each found that during those types of workouts, the mind is constantly focused on the body in order to maintain coordination and concentrate on a variety of movements in changing patterns. This can lead to a "clearing of the mind," experience that can be a great place from which to start writing.

However, both found that if they can't transition from focusing on the body and finding that rhythmic flow then they can't generally channel the creative magic that leads to aha moments regarding plot, character, and more. The act of clearing the mind (and strengthening the body) is quite valuable to overall health, but the benefit of solving writing problems through walking requires a smooth, consistent movement. It is an experience that can be taken far beyond our Mindful Writers Retreats or solo walks at home. We share this gift now with authors across time and place. And that is indeed a miracle.

"Don't panic. Midway through writing a novel, I have regularly experienced moments of bowel-curdling terror, as I contemplate the drivel on the screen before me and see beyond it, in quick succession, the derisive reviews, the friends' embarrassment, the failing career, the dwindling income, the repossessed house, the divorce . . . Working doggedly on through crises like these, however, has always got me there in the end. Leaving the desk for a while can help. Talking the problem through can help me recall what I was trying to achieve before I got stuck. Going for a long walk almost always gets me thinking about my manuscript in a slightly new way…"

~Sarah Waters

When I'm in turmoil,
when I can't think,
when I'm exhausted and afraid
and feeling very, very alone,
I go for walks.

~*Jim Butcher*, Storm Front

Emotional Journey

Breathe

Breathe

Breathe

What are all the ways that writers become frustrated and stop making progress with their work? Let's count them. Stress, worry, loss, sorrow, fear, ego, and anger can smother even the most seasoned writer's artistic urge. These negative emotions clog creative paths and make it impossible to open up to the ingenious knowledge that is already alive inside.

One way to knock out that type of writing obstacle is through mindful movement. For Kathie, this was an accidental discovery. This magic solution came while spending endless hours in the pool for swim team. An argument, a stalled homework assignment, best-times that wouldn't budge...

As she swam, these things – distractions and problems – would play through her mind until the negativity associated with the events had expended themselves, lost their energy, dried up, and fluttered away like dandelion seed taken on the wind.

Suddenly, she was invigorated to work harder or differently.

She'd find a new way to discuss a problem with her mother. The algorithm that had escaped her was now clear. She was freed up to re-approach life, mentally refreshed even if physically exhausted.

Again and again, this happened. Likewise, in college when she started running, the same thing occurred. After a good hour, her body had filtered out all that plagued her mind. She was ready to plunge back into work, back into life.

Let's look closer at how to encourage this type of cleansing.

Hanh says, "With continued mindfulness practice, you can create a peaceful space in your heart in which you can consciously embrace your feelings and emotions as you walk" (*Walking Meditation*, pp.34–35).

Wallowing in worry or fear, allowing it to stop your work, results in no progress, no joy, no *art* at all.

Lori has also found that negative feelings can hinder her progress in writing, especially pertaining to success, rejection, fear, and bad reviews.

Through walking, movement becomes a safe place to feel the negative emotions that clog the path to completing beloved projects.

To name the negative feeling, to feel it while moving, somehow allows it to be done away with, to release it, allowing it to trail behind, gone on the crisp winter wind. Perspective is altered and the mind is ready to work.

Perhaps if it was the case that focusing on a problem while walking only led to sinking into further despair, to lashing out in anger or to having progress stop by paralyzing fear, we would turn our attention away from the problem, putting attention back footfalls ONLY: one, two, three…

Instead, by acknowledging a concern, by naming it, resolution can occur. For instance, at times Kathie is overcome with panic that she's chosen the wrong professional path. Indie-publishing is lonely. The derision in the voice of fellow authors who think it's evidence she's "quit" or that the path is "less than" is palpable. Disappointment on the face of a writer who "would never," do the same can be damaging to the ego.

Breathe

Breathe

Breathe

She breathes to remember the strength of her choice, to access the core of knowing deep inside that reminds her the quality of her writing does not change depending on how it comes to market.

She takes the same care in crafting her work whether she hires the professionals who partner in bringing her writing to market, whether for a small local magazine, or for a big, powerful publishing house. She treats the process the same. She immerses in the art in the same way. The art of writing is the only element she can control, the only part that she can nurture, that she can love.

Likewise Lori finds walking to be magical and healing in so many ways. Once the rhythm of the walk and the breathing are in sync, she's discovered that focusing inward can not only spark creativity, but the process helps to erode the useless fears and self-criticism.

She finds that after a meditative walk, her self-esteem has been replenished, along with the blossoming of new story ideas. The ability to write is a gift. She acknowledges that she was chosen to tell a particular story at a particular time and no one else can tell it the same way.

The physical effects of running and walking also make Lori feel better about herself, stronger, and healthier. She gains a sense of control. She's controlling her stress, her health and therefore she's in control of her life. This high allows her to feel courageous.

Lori and Kathie have learned that disparaging comments can hinder the writing process until the negativity can be walked out, treaded over, rendering it powerless in the face of what is really true.

They can write. They will write. Until dealt with, the fear will collect in the throat, clotted with threads of *what if, what if, what if.*

There was a time Kathie didn't recognize that as fear and it drew her away from her work, from all the gifts that come with meditative movement. Now, she names it. *I am scared, I am scared, I am scared,* while moving. And before very long, there is a calming, a knowing that in writing, she is doing what she was meant to do. She is who she is supposed to be.

> *Breathe*
>
> *Breathe*
>
> *Breathe*

Author Sarah Waters has expressed similar thoughts and experiences in regard to her writing process. "Midway through writing a novel, I have regularly experienced moments of bowel-curdling terror." Like many writers, Waters gets caught worrying about all the ways her book will fail. It starts a chain of events that render her life unrecognizable, and not in any of the good ways people fantasize about.

Waters has a store of solutions for dealing with this murky middle portion of her writing process including taking walks to freshen her stale view of the work-in-progress.

We are not alone.

Breathe

Breathe

Breathe

Creative Action—Part 1:

If plagued with self-doubt, try this meditation before walking:

I am grateful for the miracle of this human body, the magic of the heart pumping blood to every organ, for my lungs filling with air over and over.

No one can extinguish my creative spark with their unkind words.

Rejection is a part of writing and it does not define me. Rejection makes me a better writer. Criticism only fuels me.

I feel my thoughts rise above the petty negative internal talk, and I can now focus on the gifts I've been given.

After some stretching, begin your walk. Now walking, picking up speed, turn attention inward; all fear leaves. Think: *It is gone, it is gone, it's gone.* Through movement, the despair is noticed and freed instead of captured inside to strangle hope, suffocate perseverance, squash joy. Admit the fear. Open up to the feeling of *I'm scared, I'm scared, I am scared.* And then, as though the fear were a sugarloaf left in the rain, it will be gone.

Creative Action Part 2:

If you're feeling down during your walk, consciously tell the negative feelings to leave, or focus on positive feelings that negate the bad ones (good reviews, readers who love your writing, and other positive things that have come out of your writing life/projects).

Focus on your work-in-progress and work through a scene, or if your particular negative feeling that day was, let's say, fear of poor book sales, then focus on creating new ways to market those books, eliciting positive thoughts – the opposite of this day's particular fear.

I give to the Universe, and the Universe gives to me.

Breathe

Breathe

Breathe

Back to the Body…Back to the Breath… Back to the Book.

If you seek creative ideas,
go walking.
Angels whisper to a man
when he goes for a walk.

~Raymond I. Myers

A Writer's High

"Exercise induces changes in mental status, particularly analgesia, sedation, anxiolysis, and a sense of wellbeing" (Dietrich, McDaniel, *Journal of Sports Medicine,* 2004). This description captures a clinical characterization that athletes of every skill level relate when they suggest their chosen activity has lulled them into an intoxicating, lovely, addictive sensation that makes all the hard work, the pain they pushed through, worth it.

They are floating; they are rewarded internally (even if not in any external way) for pushing themselves past a level of discomfort that causes other exercisers to surrender. They're high.

Writers also experience a similar intoxication when finishing a draft, plugging plot holes, or accomplishing a day of steady progress.

Any sport that requires repetitive movement (rather than teamwork like basketball or lacrosse) has enthusiasts who will attest to the endorphins that kick in. Their chemistry alters the mind, heals the heart, and invites hope back into their lives.

While the chemical evidence for this high is conclusive, and addictive – making the runner or walker want to chase that feeling – it's the creative high that is most enticing for artists and writers.

Most writers have felt the same "floating" feeling when writing as the exercisers do when running. Kathie feels it especially while writing first drafts. Nearly every day of first-draft writing, Kathie can count on that sensation. But as she delves into revision and struggle with plot holes and uncharacteristic character behavior, she turns to walking to create that joy, to prod the process and reveal the solutions.

Lori also experiences that same rush mid-walk once she's unclogged the mental debris and allowed her characters to interact in a way she did not expect. Her character may reveal something new, and this is exciting. Or, she'll feel it when a certain writing block finally breaks down, like the "Kool-aid man" busting through a wall. Or a plot bridge appears, helping her tie a key scene to the next.

This euphoria intensifies when she returns to her laptop and drafts a new scene or fixes a problem. The positive effects of this "high" can be felt throughout the day.

When she's not writing, but simply thinking about her work-in-progress, those same feelings will begin to flutter. She's equated these flutters to feelings of when we first fall in love. They are the resurfacing of hope, or the feeling that something exciting is about to happen.

This endorphin release often occurs while sitting at the computer, but for times when the slog of a stalled manuscript is too much to bear, a walk in the fresh air changes things significantly.

When a writer walks, arms swinging, legs picking up speed, she can encourage that endorphin release and this can help her back to her computer, refreshed and ready to tackle the work again.

Often, the walk not only produces the endorphins needed to lift the mood and clear the mind, but the meditative state can shake loose the manuscript problem. *Solvitur ambulando* – it is solved by walking. Trust this. Try it.

Creative Action:

Write down a list of what brings you feelings of euphoria, happy flutters, or joy during your writing process. Think of all of the ways writing makes you happy. Whenever you're feeling down, wanting to quit, or plagued with negative thoughts, refer back to this list. This is why you love to write so use this as a motivation to keep writing. Then, go for a long meditative walk and know that by the end, you'll be feeling all the feels once again.

All truly great thoughts
are conceived while walking

~Friedrich Nietzsche

Unglued

Researchers from Tufts and Stanford Universities found "fluid movement enhanced creativity in three domains: creative generation, cognitive flexibility, and the ability to make remote connections" (Slepian & Ambady, 2012).

Although the study did not examine writing specifically, and the fluid movement in the study was not walking (this will be discussed later), the findings still apply. The three creative domains mentioned above are at the heart of the work writers do each day.

Let's take the first domain – creative generation. Walking greatly enhances a writer's ability to generate ideas. For Kathie, this is especially the case with first drafts. That's always been her favorite part of writing. Her easy, relatively prolific output is encouraged, naturally, by her running/walking habits.

Without much strain, she belts out a first draft; the ideas barrel out after morning walks. When starting a book, she might create a music playlist that gets at the tone, time, and characters in the book. After walking, she heads home and thousands of words arrive shortly after brewing the coffee.

We hate to use that word *magic* again, but that's how it feels.

After the fun of first draft awesomeness, it's easy to imagine that the next steps in the writing process left Kathie wishing it only took one draft to finish a book. For many years, revision, more revision, and editing made her hobble along a plodding, uninspiring, sometimes awful path, with a heaviness hanging over the process. Though there are some writers who come out of one draft with a fully realized manuscript, most find that using the creative domains of cognitive flexibility and making or fine-tuning remote connections – the skills that make a manuscript sing – occur in later writing cycles.

Kathie didn't realize at first that meditative practice could make the part of her brain that handles cognitive inflexibility more supple, more able to fill in the empty hollows of contrived solutions, creating unique finishes and "life-like" characters. With the help of mindful walking and sitting meditation, being conscious of their power and tapping into it over the years, she found that Slepian and Ambady's cognitive flexibility and making remote connections could be honed and used like any tool in a skilled cobblers belt. These days, she finds elements of revision as exhilarating as drafting.

Meditative walking encourages flexibility, to trust that just because the sentence written in that first draft was once considered the most powerful sentiment ever crafted, it might not fit in later drafts at all. Practicing mindfulness allows writers to understand that the right way to express the idea will come. The original can be released.

This condition of being "glued" to what's written actually causes discomfort. The mental pain encountered in making changes isn't usually rooted in ego or the thought that the work was correct or finished. It's that when a mind is less developed than it should be, the writer cannot imagine they have the ability to preserve the idea they hold dear but change the way it's presented, so it can work with the rest of the story. Fear of changing one thing, worrying that the alteration will ruin the rest and put the manuscript even further from completion, can cause writers to bristle and become surly.

Mindful walking is one antidote. Through its practice, thoughts and steadfast ideas will yield and stretch and make room for the character who really belonged in the book, the plot element that should be set free, the language that was all wrong for Rose, even though Kathie really, really wanted it to be right.

Lori, too, found that she was becoming too rigid in not wanting to change things that weren't quite working. When her critique group once suggested the reworking of – what she believed to be – an important scene, she became anxious and almost paralyzed. After stepping away from the problem, taking a walk and honing back into the practice of mindfulness, a light bulb went off. She started drafting the old scene in a new way, and it was so much better than before. That situation taught her not to hold tightly to drafted material. Change is not only good, but often times it's so much better.

The same transformation happens in terms of becoming better at making remote connections. Plot, plot, plot. The ability to see creative solutions and unique connections in a story is often tied directly to plot.

Walking invites your mind to grow supple and far more creative over the years. Let the fluid movement open your mind, enrich your work and reveal the plot twist you hadn't seen coming until it pops into your mind fully formed, transported on the wings of one of those fluttering bluebirds you noticed landing on the riverbank the other day.

- Creative generation
- Cognitive flexibility
- Remote connections

These creative domains are in play whether you write fiction or nonfiction. An article writer who struggles with structure or flow or finding the heart inside all the hard facts will benefit in all the same ways as fiction writers. At the center of every type of writing, is an author's soul and for that reason, creativity is at the center of any manuscript.

Creative Action:

With all her years of mindful walking, Lori has the ability to choose a particular problem to solve (for instance, how to get Claire and Marcus to meet in the next scene). Once she's into her walking or running, she considers the scene prior to her problem area and lets the characters talk.

Try interviewing yourself as you walk: *What are you trying to accomplish with this scene? What's the purpose of that conversation? How is this carrying the theme? How does it move the plot?* Then, direct the interview to the character: *Claire, how are you feeling in this scene? What are your fears? How did you feel when you first met Marcus? Describe it to me.*

Like Lori, you can train yourself to focus on a particular plot issue or dialogue exchange that you're struggling with. Other times, Lori simply reminds herself:

Body, Breath, Book… and the openness invites all sorts of solutions and creative twists on stories as old as time.

My only comfort is in motion.

~*Charles Dickens*

Exercise for Mental & Writing Health

You may be wondering why we've included a section on mental health in a walking meditation book. We think optimism and a positive outlook are tied directly to writing. It is a leap of faith when a writer unveils his inner world even if it's through fiction. It takes guts to lay a body of work open to an audience, to be loved or... not.

We think there is a seed of hope in each author that grows its sprouts when needed most. When writers wonder if they'll be rejected yet again – if they have the time, the energy, the skill to start again – that is when the seed sprouts and reminds us... *Yes, keep on. This is what you are meant to do.* Artists don't sow that seed themselves, it's just there, ready to provide energy to tired words.

But it certainly helps to nurture the seed, to allow in the light that encourages it to grow so it can, in turn, encourage us to write on.

A writing journey, this *writing migration* that is tethered to a *walking journey*, provides an important safety net for writers and artists.

Writers are sensitive. This is good. This is what allows them to notice the way a friend says she's okay, but her eyes dart to the floor and she turns away before explaining why her words don't match her body language. Creatives (and this includes nonfiction writers as well) often absorb other people's sorrow; they feel other people's pain.

An author describing her journey to success as a self-employed businesswoman will excavate her past and experience emotions and events she may have forgotten about. A journalist who delves into the lives of cancer warriors or those who've experienced violence will carry these emotions as he writes. This is part of what enriches their work. Writers can shape scenes that leave readers in tears because they can imagine or "call up" the pain of heartbreak or a loved one's death or the sizzling heights of first love.

All the observing, feeling, and the gathering of poignant, moving moments that give artists the ability to produce their work can also darken their moods, altering the way they see the world and leaving them emotionally depleted. It's important for writers to protect themselves from being overwhelmed by their own depression, worry, and fear.

Some artists seem to have Teflon skin. Nothing negative even gets inside their heads. Others can segregate their thoughts or the judgment of others from their feelings. But many are affected by rejection, bad reviews, or the lack of enthusiasm from a loved one. Walking meditation is one way (in addition to professional mental health assistance) to help keep a writer on track and to shore up his resistance to all the emotional stuff that churns the very air he breathes.

A report called "Understanding Depression" published by Harvard Health Publications (pg. 35) discussed the body of literature that very clearly points to regular exercise being as potent as prescription drugs for managing "mild to moderate depression." Also, the article indicates that people who continued to exercise regularly are less likely to find themselves battling depression again.

This information is not intended to replace the care of a licensed physician or alter anyone's medical treatment, but it's worth considering that writers could make use of this powerful tool to help their writing, and possibly improve their health.

Creative Action:

While under the care of a professional or for a minor pick-me-up, force yourself out for a walk. Or pull out the yoga mat and stretch, catching a rhythm as you slide from pose to pose. Fresh air, a dirt path, even a busy sidewalk can lend to an uplifting moment that allows a struggling writer to see the world in a new way.

Do the same stretching as before (page 19). While stretching, or in between moves, recite this meditation:

> *I acknowledge I'm not feeling my best today, but I'll walk anyway.*
>
> *My (joints) are achy and my (back) isn't feeling great, but I'll walk anyway.*
>
> *Clear my mind of all the clutter and worries, and let my body heal.*
>
> *May each breath heal my body.*
>
> *May each footfall clear my mind.*
>
> *Today, I will walk anyway and be grateful for this time with nature.*
>
> *I give to the universe and the universe gives to me.*
>
> *I deserve to feel the joy of writing. I deserve the healing that comes from creating.*
>
> *I will reach out to a friend later, or call my doctor, if I'm still not feeling well.*

Let me walk. Let me breathe. Let me feel joy. Let me create.

Back to my body, back to my breath, back to my book.

I would walk along the Quais
[...] when I was trying to
think something out.
It was easier to think
if I was walking...

~Ernest Hemingway,
A Moveable Feast

Zen and the Art of Cognitive Maintenance

Okay, so you're still not convinced that walking could help your writing? Well, it seems every person over the age of thirty-two laments his mental acuity, his ability to remember all that was once easy to recall on demand while doing handstand beer shooters.

A writer's heart, soul, and life are his source material, but it takes the mind to weave intricate threads of story so a tale rivets readers to the page, sending them whipping through the book.

"Greater amounts of walking are associated with greater gray matter volume, which is in turn associated with a reduced risk of cognitive impairment" (Erickson, Raji, Lopez, Becker, Rosano, Newman, Gach, Thompson, Ho, and Kuller, *Neurology* 2010). That's right. According to Erickson et al.'s findings, the brains of people who walked were significantly larger nine years later. Yes, you may be thinking, "But I'm only twenty-four (or thirty-seven, forty-eight)," or what have you… but don't you want to get a jump on things while you're young? Yes. The answer's yes. Save that brain matter. Move your feet.

If a pitch man on late-night TV promised a product that could make you high, keep you young, and help you fulfill your life's calling, wouldn't you listen? Just for a second? It would seem too good to be true, yes, but with all this evidence, with all these authors saying "this free thing, available to anyone willing to take the opportunity, can work," isn't it worth a try?

Creative Action:

Try this on a day you're just not feeling it.

Start with some light stretching. Breathe in, breathe out, and recite this meditation:

> *I don't want to walk today, but I deserve it.*
>
> *I deserve to feel good. I deserve to feel the lightness that follows a brisk walk. I deserve to feel the joy of creating today.*
>
> *I deserve to feel the breeze on my skin, the cool chill in the air, and to hear the birds singing.*
>
> *I feel my breath fill my lungs. In and out. I can imagine my body getting stronger as the blood courses quicker with each step. I am stronger with each breath. In and out. Stronger with each step.*

I feel my body come alive. I am stronger, I am more creative, I am one with nature.

I give to the universe.

The universe gives to me.

Back to my body, back to my breath, back to my book.

The Americans *never* walk.
In winter too cold
and in summer too hot.

~J.B. Yeats

Waiting for the Weather

Yeah. Stop that – waiting for the perfect weather. Stop whining and complaining about how the cold or the heat or rain is keeping you from walking. We love Yeats's quote. We all have our weather preferences and hopefully we get to live in an area of the world where the climate makes us happy and comfortable. But it's likely that some portion of the year will leave you squinting away from snow squalls that send icy knives into your cheeks, chilling you to the marrow.

Other times, thick, woolen heat makes it hard to draw a full breath under the midday sun. We say, make it work. With safety taken into account of course (we're not talking about pushing through an ultra-marathon on the hottest day of summer – grab your lemonade and read a book on the porch that day!) get outside, get moving, get those ideas curdling so you can pluck one, insert it into your work-in-progress and turn your blah manuscript into the magnificent tome it was meant to be.

Kathie hates the heat. She's got Multiple Sclerosis and all it takes is for the temperature to rise above 75 degrees and the dew-point temperature to scale past

61, and her energy will be sapped, mental acuity blunted. It's as though her body is rotting from the inside out. It sucks. But the fact that her health stinks on some level doesn't mean she can't make use of one of the greatest writing tools she knows.

So, in the heat of summer, she makes sure that most days, she walks early or late in the day. She'll still walk midday if she absolutely needs to, but just like she makes time to actually sit in front of her computer, she also makes time to walk. It's imperative to her writing process.

Most complaints about walking seem to come in the winter. But with all the advancements in cold-weather clothing, it is possible for a person to walk around the Arctic in snow pants, hat, gloves, and coat and still feel temperate. It will at least be possible for a writer to take a walk for an hour in 25 degrees (okay, 10 degrees... go out even if it's 10 degrees!) before heading back in to the desk.

The winter quiet is amazing. The snowy blanket that insulates and absorbs city sounds and leaves the writer enveloped in thoughts, the crunching of snow a metronomic accompaniment that lures stubborn thoughts out of hiding.

The smell of winter is clean. Its crisp gales rush over exposed skin and put nerves on edge, bringing an artist's attention to the immediate world, to all the ways a winter walk may influence wintertide writing.

It is true: a safe place to walk in the winter is imperative. No one wants to finish their book with their foot in traction. But there are places that are nearly always ready and welcoming for winter walkers. The zoo is one. There are miles of pathways and all are plowed and ice-free. There are few people at the zoo in the winter (*Shhh*, don't tell anyone else) and it's rife with inspirational sights and sounds. Or try the mall, just as it opens or closes, for a huge loop that's flat and safe.

Lori also is not a fan of the heat. She loves the tranquility of a quiet snowy day. For those who do not agree, Lori would like to share that some of her best endorphin rushes have come following a run or a long walk in inclement weather. She's signed up for quite a few 5K runs and they've mostly happened in cold or even snow and rain. But the rewards afterward were well worth the initial discomfort. There's something to be said for proving your mental endurance and literally walking outside of your comfort zone.

Invest in a pair of snowshoes. Sauntering over a foot-high snowy dale can bring to bear a tsunami of ideas. The payoff? A great writing session to follow, right by the fireplace, with coffee or hot chocolate in hand. In this case, be un-American. Show Yeats we have changed… Find a way to work the winter walking into your process.

Creative Action Part 1:

Try this when the weather is not ideal.

Who wants to get a good dose of endorphins? First, dress warmly, or put on the rain poncho, and let's get moving, so our creativity will be at its best. Once you're all ready to go, do some light stretching. Breathe in and breath out, and recite this meditation:

> *The air is cool (or rainy or snowy) but it is still a majestic work of mother nature. I want to be one with nature and experience her in all of her glory.*
>
> *Today's weather was chosen for a purpose and a reason, and I want to experience it. I deserve to experience it and I am grateful for this day.*
>
> *As my breath moves into my lungs... and out... I feel myself preparing to face all of the wondrous elements.*
>
> *Like my emotions, weather is fleeting. I want to experience it, embrace it, and learn from it. But it cannot stifle my joy or my creative flow. It will enhance it. It will bring the summer and spring that's inside of me to the surface.*
>
> *I feel stronger with each breath. I feel stronger with each step. I am one with the universe and with nature.*
>
> *The universe gives to me, and I give to the universe.*

I deserve the joy and the high I will feel as my blood pumps through my veins and the creative thoughts begin to bloom.

Back to my body, back to my breath, back to my book.

Creative Action Part 2:

Every protagonist experiences pain, suffering or discomfort at some point. Use the unpleasant moments during your walk in inclement weather to tap into feelings your characters may experience during moments of suffering. Jot down any new sensations or reactions that you may want to use in future descriptions in your writing.

Creative Action Part 3:

Keep a notebook of the rhythms of your winter walking – especially if you hate it. Kathie does this for summer walking so she can feel as though she accomplished something when she sees that yes, high humidity and an MS flare kept her from walking every day that week, but she was able to walk every other day. With the notation about not feeling well and the results that the mindfulness yielded in her writing that week she could only call it a success even if not ideal.

The only friend to walk with
is one who so exactly
shares your taste
for each mood of the countryside
that a glance, a halt,
or at most a nudge,
is enough to assure that the
pleasure is shared.

~C. S. Lewis

Walking with Company

Walking and running with others can be inspiring. As a Ph.D. student, Kathie ran regularly with classmates and professors. Keeping the same pace, the pounding over pavement, they shared an experience that led to easy conversation. Research questions were raised and possible methodology was explored. Solutions were found and camaraderie deepened.

A 2013 *Huffington Post* article by Arianna Huffington indicated that when it was possible she "would have hiking meetings instead of sit-down meetings." In that same article, psychologist Laurel Lippert Fox stated that she meets with patients and walks with them throughout the appointment.

When Lori runs or walks with friends, she doesn't garner the same problem-solving experience as when she's alone, unless they're all walking in silence, with the same end goal. Walking alone or finding partners who are comfortable in moving through silence, who understand that the accompaniment of breath, breeze, and footfalls are all that's needed, can be important.

Unless you're walking with others to work out issues in a collaborative project or to socialize (yes, we need to be social, too!), be sure to always cordon off some of each walk for yourself. Sometimes the cleansing walk with a friend can ignite your inspiration and pepper in the excitement you need to get back to work.

The first writing retreat Kathie attended was with the ladies of FatPlum. Judy Schneider was one of the coordinators of the weekend. Early in the morning each had gone off for a walk on their own and crossed paths at one point. It was on that walk that they first got to know each other. Walking together inspired Kathie's work that weekend and beyond. It also created a friendship that lasted well over a decade.

Fellowship can be an important part of an author's writing migration. But protect your time; keep a large portion of walking for yourself so you can tend to your work in the manner it deserves.

He who limps
is still walking.

~Stanislaw J. Lec

So, you can't walk...

There are people who are unable to walk and therefore may not experience walking meditation the way it's been described here. It's still possible to garner the benefits of fluid movement without leaving your home, and if necessary, without leaving your chair.

Think back to Slepian and Ambady, the researchers who studied fluid movement and its influence on creative thought. We immediately connected their method and findings to what we experience during and as a result of walking meditation. But Slepian and Ambady didn't have their study participants walk a track or circle a lake in the woods before engaging in the study tasks. They simply had them trace drawings that either forced their hand to move fluidly or to move with stops and starts as they traced angular lines (*Journal of Experimental Psychology*, 2012). They found clear evidence that fluid movement, even that of one's hand, can enhance creative thinking. Think of that! This finding means that most people can experience moving meditation and its benefits for writing.

What does this mean for homebound writers who want to complement their sitting meditation with a fluid, moving meditation? It means it *can* be duplicated with smaller movements.

Julia Cameron is the prolific, insightful, widely read author of *The Artist's Way* and *Walking in This World: The Practical Art of Creativity*, among many, many other books. One of the tools she asks writers to use is what she calls "morning pages." In the first minutes of the day, she suggests artists take a journal and write, by hand, anything that comes to mind. She believes the movement, the fluid, cursive motion, is linked to better, richer, more focused work later in the day.

Like Cameron, Madhu Wangu incorporates journaling into the process of sitting meditation. She recognizes that though she sits, she is far from being *still*. Meditation is powerful and generative, and journaling helps capture the ideas born of meditation or prepare the writer for sitting meditation. Cameron says, "I have come to think of morning pages as a form of meditation…"

It seems that Wangu and Cameron's observations, experiences through their own practice, and feedback from fellow artists supports Slepian and Ambady's findings. The act of fluid writing gets the artistic center whirling. This is good news for writers who have mobility concerns or issues.

In addition, Thich Nhat Hanh has suggested that if people who can't take part in walking meditations use their eyes to follow the walking movements of another person, the benefits can be shared in this manner.

All of these things provide hope and alternatives for authors who want to experience the benefits of fluid movement and mindful writing.

Creative Action:

Here's a meditation for you to try if you're using alternative fluid movements:

I am grateful for all of the ways I can move my body.

I will try new things. I will experience new ways to call on my creative flow.

I feel the breath enter my lungs, and I'm grateful for it. I hear sounds around me and acknowledge them. I'm grateful for my surroundings.

I scan my body. I feel some aches, but they won't stop my flow. I am grateful for all of the parts of me that are feeling good today.

I give to the universe and the universe gives to me.

I will sketch a scene or symbol to represent something in my work-in-progress. I'll trace over and around it until my mind is still.

I will journal about the ways I am grateful today. I will journal about the blocks I want to tear down.

Back to my body, back to my breath, back to my book.

Getting Started
~ It's Simple, Just Move

Walking can bring clarity. The preceding pages indicate that not only does walking or meditative movement sharpen one's thoughts, but it can be a wellspring for layered, rich writing.

The quotes scattered among the book show that this meditative writing experience has been enjoyed by authors the world over, dating back centuries. But to writers who haven't tried it before, it may seem simply crazy rather than simple.

Like Lori and Kathie, many writers have stumbled upon this meditative state because they were runners who found their mind entered a peaceful state, a flexible problem-solving condition, once their bodies entered fluid, automated movement.

Like Thich Nhat Hanh, some have found a slow walk or quiet swim in the early morning hours can bring a sense of peace that creates fertile ground for creation and progress in their work.

So, how does one start this? Websites like MeditationOasis.com provide step-by-step instructions for how to begin walking meditation. Instructions should be used as jumping off points, or guidelines.

But adhering to a strict process of movement can become constricting, perhaps counterproductive. Looking for exactness in walking meditation may stop a new practitioner from continuing on, from reaping the benefits that are waiting.

Like a hiker who must cross a rope bridge spanning a deep gorge, wondering if it will hold, if he can get across when the ropes and planks seem unfathomably fragile, the writer must just take the first step and trust the bridge will hold. Trust that through walking, through opening up to fluid movement, the mind will follow. The solutions, the inspiration, the richness will come.

Don't force it. Court it. Walking brings your muse.

Notice your steps, the sky, your breath.

Body. Breath. Book.

Breathe

Breathe

Breathe

Creative Action:

While walking, it's normal for your mind to wander away from your work-in-progress. Acknowledge the random thoughts and associated feelings they may bring, and send them away for another time. You will deal with that later. This is writing time. Now is a good time to repeat your favorite mantra or try out a new one. Or, repeat:

I give to the Universe and the Universe gives to me.

Focus on your footfalls, then on your breathing, syncing them if possible (3 steps, inhale, 3 steps, exhale). Then, repeat:

Back to the body,
back to the breath,
back to the book…

Next, hone in on your scene and your character. What do you want to accomplish in this scene? Ask your character some questions. If there is more than one character in the scene, let them talk to each other… even if it's unplanned and doesn't pertain to the scene. Have fun and let the ideas begin to flow.

Breathe in, breathe out.
Body. Breath. Book…

Make your feet your friend.

~*James Barrie*

The Bridge

Bridges must be one of the greatest and deceptively simple engineering designs known to man. Every day we cross them metaphorically and literally. They allow us to tie pieces of life together to best suit our needs.

Sometimes it takes a concrete example to help inform a meditative practice like mindful writing. Lori, Kathie, and two other retreaters, Denise and Audrey, had the chance to experience the marvel of a simple cable bridge across a cold rushing creek while at the Spring 2016 Mindful Writers Retreat. It was the fourth such event but only the second one held at the Ligonier site, so they were still getting familiarized with Laurel Mountain.

The retreat center was doing some tree maintenance on the trails they'd used the time before. The director pointed them in a different direction for walking, away from the woods. At first sight this took them down toward the main road and didn't seem as though it would lend the same heavenly walk in the woods that the trails above did. But they made the best of it. As instructed they headed toward Mona's

Run, watching first light glow through the trees along the road as they moved, still not sure where they were going. The fringes of dawn were starting to peel back, revealing brilliant blue sky. The twenty-three degree air invigorated them. They skirted a large field and found Mona's Run, satisfied that they wouldn't have to walk along the road. But a little further into the woods they saw there was no way across the water. They groaned at the thought their mindful walk had ended less than twenty minutes into it. Disappointed, they explored in the still darkness a little more, winding along the stream bed a little further and saw *it*. With the sun just barely up—was it really there? Strung across the bustling Mona's Run was a bridge! Well, not a bridge like they'd normally experienced. It was a wobbly, cable contraption with two braided metal strands to hold and a single length to tightrope walk across. The sense of excitement that there was a way – that their walk was not over – filled them. Like it been drawn from the pages of a fairy tale, there was an answer.

They rushed toward it. None of them was sure of making it without falling into the frigid water, but each crossed, breath held, one hesitant footstep in front of the other, holding the cable handrails as they wiggled, bending and shaking. There was no way for anyone to assist the other across the bridge. They felt as though they were on a high wire. The rising sun lit the water on fire, diamonds leaping and jumping on the surface. It was absolutely incredible.

In those moments and upon reflection later, they realized that when it comes to writing, there's always a bridge to the next word, sentence, career phase, even when it isn't readily noticeable. They learned that going a little further, looking for unexpected bridges over the obstacles, is inherently part of mindful walking. If you get out and move, the bridges to solutions reveal themselves.

This book is a bridge between walking meditation and sitting meditation. They work in tandem to enrich writing. Some weeks you may find you utilize sitting meditation more than walking. Perhaps you begin your day with sitting meditation and then need to walk during the afternoon as problems in your manuscript arise.

What obstacles in your writing life or manuscript require a bridge for you to continue on your path? Can you trust that the bridge will appear?

There is so much more to relate about walking meditation. This little book only presents a sliver of the research tied to practice. This book offers a way to get started. Use it in parts or in whole. Keep a journal to illustrate the patterns of your life that feed and starve your writing life. Make mindful walking a part of it.

And for those looking for more, here are some topics that might help bridge where you are as a mindful writer to where you want to go:

- Music and meditation
- Competing concentration
- Night walking
- Small walking spaces – pacing

Just as people are told to listen to their bodies when it comes to the amount of food or drink they consume, you should do the same when it comes to using meditative tools. There are times writers just know they need to get up and go walk, that the movement will shed light on what is wrong with the work. Listen for those whispers, notice that feeling associated with needing to move and then respond.

Lori and Kathie can't wait to hear about your experiences and hope that you are willing to share them as a learning community.

There is no right or wrong with walking meditation. It may take time to experience all that has been written here. But commit to it for a time and see what happens. Iain Sinclair, a writer for whom walking is of enormous importance, categorizes authors as *those who walk* and *those who don't*. He says that walking writers are those "who definitely have, within their writing, this rhythm of journeys and walks and pilgrimages and quests" (Coverley, 2012).

Whether writing fiction or nonfiction, this type of enrichment of one's work – a lyricism of sorts – is well worth the time it takes to find your way back to writing through walking.

Please enjoy the following poems written by Madhu Wangu. They capture the ebb and flow of the writing process and will help prepare you for the work ahead! Enjoy them throughout reading this book and beyond.

And remember…

Breathe

Breathe

Breathe

Body – Breath – Book

The Poems

By *Madhu Bazaz Wangu*

Madhu Wangu's wisdom and practice informs many writers' journeys. Use her poems or a piece of one to replace a mantra or meditation or simply enjoy as they are.

Simply Write!

Simply write!

Do not speak of your writing.

Do not speak of other people's writings.

Do not speak of the business of writing.

Sit still in silence and solitude.

When body, heart and mind are one,

When your senses have moved inward,

Let the stream flow.

Unravel your knots in spontaneous words.

Other writer's success or failure does not affect you.

Profit or loss does not touch you.

Praise or criticism does not ruffle you.

Derive pleasure solely from writing.

Experience the bliss.

Simply write!

The Writer and The Creator

Don't get tangled in outer reality,

Or get caught in inner.

Be true to both.

Make distinction.

Once you plant yourself deep within,

Knots and tangles unravel by themselves.

Keep your intention alive!

Return to the source often.

Focus on intention. There is insight in acting.

The act will envelope you with bliss.

No obstacles. No blocks.

When you let go, things happen of themselves.

When sensations, thoughts and feelings coalesce into one

rough drafts of thousands of words are born.

There you are, in the book.

There is the Self, in the book.

When you realize this,

Nothing but unshakable security, deep bliss.

Writing Alone Together

On the path to completing a manuscript

I write alone with other writers.

Each one of us absorbed within by the magnificent power of writing together

Writing authentically without desire, fear or guilt

We endeavor to excavate memories and reveal insights.

In silence

In stillness

In solitude

We sit to write with our authentic voices.

The inner voice asks:

Why do you write?

What is the purpose?

I say:

To remember my memories

to harvest my imagination

To harness my insights

To know myself

If I receive, I rejoice.

If I don't, I continue to practice.

I let go of desire for fame and success.

This is the secret of my joy, our joy.

Door of Opportunity

A careless critique from a fellow writer?
Return hers with honest comments.

"Here," she hands you the draft, "the weak parts highlighted!"
Show her where her strengths lie.

He grabs the opportunity that was rightfully yours.
Congratulate him on his success.

By critiquing honestly,
By learning from your own strengths and skills,
By preparing through tough circumstances,
Attain the strength no one else can.

When you are ready inward,
The door of opportunity opens only for you.

Mind that Practices Mindful Writing

More than the authors you envy, more than all writers you compete against

Your chaotic mind does greater harm.

More than mentors and models, more than writing partners, more than beta readers mind that practices Mindful Writing does greater good.

Weaving the Mantra

My mantra: Revise the Day!

I weave it on the loom of my mind.

And let the joy and grace course through me.

I weave it as the sun and moon watch.

I whisper it for the sun and moon to hear.

I recite it and retain it in the lotus of my heart.

I weave it on the loom of my mind

to shape my life of ten thousand days,

to comb the twists and knots of my hundred thousand thoughts.

No more shall I weave a garment of regrets and worries.

For peace has come to me, drawn by weaving—

by ceaselessly lacing the mantra on the loom of my mind.

No time is to be set, no action needed,

for weaving it.

for chanting it.

Listen!

Breathe!

In

Out

In

Out

In

Out

In stillness, listen!

Listen to Self reveal itself.

That dwells within and never ceases to be.

Listen with awareness and openness.

Listen to the silent voice.

Listen to the secret of what is and what is not.

Its flow never ceases.

Its trust never diminishes.

It never changes.

Most are too impatient to hear the voice that speaks to us from within.

Instead of saying, "How wonderful!"

Go within to experience the Infinite in all its wonder.

Who is She?

Follow her daily and you never stray from your path.

Hear her voice and your imagination thrives.

Heed her always and you face no obstacles on your way.

When she leads you you're fearless.

When she entices you you're energized.

When she courses through you you're tireless.

When she graces you reach your goal.

Make this house of blood and bones her abode.

Who is She?

Your creative flow.

Your inner voice.

Your Authentic Self.

Mindful Writing

I sit still in solitude.

Same place. Same time.

A silence speaks to me.

It speaks of complete surrender,

to feelings,

to thoughts,

to muses.

Feelings flow,

Shift me to my fictional dream.

I scribe in silence.

Yesterday's suffering transforms into compassion.

Yesterday's trial into today's courageous act.

Yesterday's transgression into redemption.

The dream has no second,

mind-born from the source within.

The Creative Source

Only few writers hear the inner voice.

Fewer still pay heed to what they have heard.

Fortunate is the Mindful Writer who listens to the Self.

Rare are those who mull over what was spoken.

Blessed are those who make Self an illumined teacher.

The intellect does only half the work. It can never touch the Self.

The Self is beyond perception,

Hidden in the lotus of the heart,

The Self is above pain and pleasure.

The Self is neither body nor heart or mind

But the three melded as one.

That One is the principle of creativity, of existence.

It is the source of aesthetic pleasure and abiding bliss.

Once stirred it can never go dormant.

Mindful writer sits still in silence and solitude,

Self within may journey far away.

Moving everything everywhere it brings back influences.

When the writers realize the Self within,

Abstractions flow in the midst of forms,

Conflict changes into growth and growth to transformation.

Sorrow moves beyond sorrows.

The Self can be known through writing, hard reading, listening.

Through disciplining and practicing skill and craft.

Through Writing Meditation Practice.

Writers Know Thyself!

Self is the inner companion enshrined in the core of your heart.

Swifter than thought,

Transcending all.

One moment away.

Abyss away.

Self is within holding your universe together.

Deny knowing the Self, remain enveloped by the darkness of your sight.

Deny knowing the Self, remain devoid of the joy.

Know this truth by the practice of daily Writing Meditation.

Know this by meditating, by walking, by journaling.

Oh writer! Stay yoked to the Self.

Remember what is at the core of your heart.

Practice Writing Meditation

Enter the realm of imagination.

Stay with the flow of creativity.

Receive insights with your eyes closed.

Cross the sea of fear.

The body turns dust but your books are immortal.

Yoking to the Flow

Sheer silence dwells in the lotus of my heart.

It brings to awareness what lays concealed inside,

Stimulates scribblings that stream as the joyous writing.

The flow yokes me to the universal consciousness,

Revealing myself to me.

Writers Write. Readers Read.

Write!

Write alone!

Let the vital energy emanate from you.

Write with others.

Feel charged with the collective energy.

Write!

Go on a quest. Conquer demons. Find the elixir.

Narrate the experience,

As a gift to your readers.

Read!

Reinvigorate the energy that exudes.

Rejoice in the gift.

Connect with the writer, the giver.

Connect with the glorious energy beyond...

beyond the writer,

beyond the reader...

To the timeless creative act.

Writing Mindfully

Who writes the stuff to which I sign my name?
Who whispers behind the mask?
What gushes forth during moments of somnolence
then sidles back swiftly wherever it comes from?

Sliding down my arm to my fingertips,
I transcribe truths in burning words.
Raptured, I write until my wrist hurts.
I stop when whisper leaves for its hidden abode.

Where does this recluse hide, whom does It abide?
It comes and returns on its free will.
It writes the word, the line, the prose, the poem.
I only attach my name to what It scribes.

Resources

Cameron, Julia. *Walking in This World: The Practical Art of Creativity*. Penguin, 2003.

Coverley, Merlin. *The Art of Wandering: The Writer as Walker*. Oldcastle Books, 2012.

Hanh, Thich Nhat. *Peace is Every Step: The Path of Mindfulness in Everyday Life*. Bantam, 1992.

_____. *The Long Road Turns to Joy: A Guide to Walking Meditation*. Parallax, 2011.

_____, and Anh-Huong Nguyen. *Walking Meditation: Easy Steps to Mindfulness*. Sounds True, 2019.

Huffington, Arianna. "Hemingway, Thoreau, Jefferson, and the Virtues of a Good Long Walk," *Huffington Post,* August 29, 2013.

Miller, Michael Craig and Julie Corliss. *Understanding Depression*. Harvard Health Publications, 2017.

Slepian, Michael L. and Nalini Ambady. "Fluid Movement and Creativity," *Journal of Experimental Psychology: General, 141*(4), pp. 625–629, 2012.

www.ingramcontent.com/pod-product-compliance
Lightning Source LLC
Chambersburg PA
CBHW020542080526
44583CB00013B/951